WILL JONES' SPACE ADVENTURES & The Zadrilian Queen ©

The Play

By: Christine Thompson-Wells

Charities

The Play

Will Jones'

Space Adventures
&
The Zadrilian Queen

By Christine Thompson-Wells

First published 2008
Second edition 2017
Third edition 2020
Copyright© Christine Thompson-Wells
All rights reserved

ISBN: 978-0-6481884-0-7

BOOKS
FOR READING
ONLINE

Published by Books For Reading On Line.Com

Overview of the story so far:

Will has been working all day long for the farmer on the Island of Ozimoth.

One good thing about the day, thought Will as he rode his bike home: 'Today is payday'. The farmer had paid Will the same amount of money as he usually paid him, but this time, the farmer had given Will a 10% bonus because he had really worked hard for the last two weeks.

Will was busily thinking about the bonus and wanted to know how much money the farmer had paid him. He was thinking too hard and suddenly, while riding his bike on the way home, he has an accident – Will comes off his bike and finds he is lying on the grass at the side of the gravel road next to a field.

While he was trying to collect his thoughts, after the accident and still lying on the grass, Will thinks he hears the familiar sound of a space ship's motor.

He is right, he does!

Will, joins the Grigan Leader and his guards and they journey to the Planet of Grigan. While on Grigan, Will takes an un-expected journey to the Planet of Zadril.

Scene One takes place when Will is hurtling down the large, black hole under the large tree on the Planet of Grigan!

Contents

Will Jones' Space Adventures
& The Zadrilian Queen©

Cast: 30 to 35 Children consisting:
            Narrator
            Zadrilian children
            Epahs people
            Lizard Woman (Queen Irdzla of Zadril)
            Princess Eex
            Elderly Zadrilian Butler
            Grigan Leader
            5 Xannnts
            Intergalactic Space Master
            Ancient Ancestor
            Mummified Ancient One

Playing
time: 7 x 20 minute sessions. This play is ideal
            for a progressive assembly over separate
            days or separate weeks.

Costumes: Green geometric card shapes (the larger
            the better).
            Purple face paint, (purple fabric cut in
            squares to cover the children's clothes

would be suitable) for the Zadrilian people.

Green face paint, (green fabric cut in squares to cover the children's clothes would be suitable) for the people in the City of Epahs.

Green swords for the Space Masters.

White sheet (Intergalactic Space Master), white shield, white sword, (both can be made out of cardboard)

White sheet (Mummified Ancient One) to be worn as a shroud.

Xannnt faces photocopied

Setting: Clear stage with added lighting a benefit for effects.

Props: **Large** green geometric shapes: triangles, pentagons, hexagons, heptagons, octagons, squares, parallelograms, rectangles, rhombi, circles, cubes and trapezia can be made by the children to enhance the play and used within scene one.

Polystyrene cut into ice flake shapes (something similar to a snow flake pattern) may be used in scene 3 to simulate the ice falling.

Spaceship Spaceships can be made using a variety of materials. Large cylinder cardboard containers made by wrapping sturdy card into a circle and securing, then painted or left as it is or other circular cardboards, polystyrene left over from packaging, can all make for an adventurous spaceship.

Rubbish In scene three, rubbish needs to be used and spread over the floor of the stage: old cartons and bags, broken furniture – anything that gets the message over about not taking responsibility for our surroundings will add impact in this scene.

Large quantities of Butchers' Paper. Please note: The paper is called Parchments throughout the Will Jones' stories. In scene four, Princess Eex wants to show Will just how hard she has worked on her school work. All of the work, however, is done on old, used paper. Paper that has been rubbed out and rubbed out.

Large quantities of brown paper. This paper is used by Princess Eex and Queen Irdzla for doing school work on. There is no other paper available only old worn out paper that has been used by the generations before Princess Eex was born.

Large pencils. The pencils are used as writing or drawing sticks

Large Chair Preferably a brown chair that the Elderly Zadrilian Butler can rest in during Scene Five Six and Seven.

Old books, brown paper cut into sheets, old exercise books. (Not magazines or comics. Enough are needed to make a pile in the corner of the stage.

Coins, copies are in the back of the book.

Toys for demonstration: Drum, Ball or others.

Green Stall (if available) for Will to sit on in the Library in Epahs.

Spaceship engine part. An engine part can be anything that is old and rusty (A part from an old washing machine would do.)

Resemblance of a screwdriver – one possibly made out of cardboard! **Cardoard shapes that resemble Mummies**. Children take these parts.

Lighting: Green lights are suggested for the space effects.

Characters: Will Jones
Queen of Zadril
Princess Eex
Old Zadrilian Butler
Little Brother (Brother to Princess Eex)
Ziob (A space master)
14 children (carrying large green shapes)
9 children (Purple, Zadrilian people including the Queen and Princess Eex)
3 green library workers and scribes
5 Green Space Masters
Grigan Leader
(Chorus children and adults)

(Please note: fewer characters may be used in the carrying of the shapes and some children may double up in the parts they play.)

Scene One:

Narrator: Will falls and falls and falls down the dark, black hole!

The scene takes place within a darkened stage with Will and Ziob performing for the major part of the scene. The children enter carrying large, green geometric shapes and singing the Part Song.

Background: As the ground moved it suddenly started to break open into a large hole within the ground. Will tries to grab the branches of the trees to stop him falling. It was too late, the branches moved further and further from his grasp. He then tries to grab the huge tree roots but soon he

1

falls past them falling, falling, deeper and deeper into the very large black hole.

Stage Direction: *The stage lighting is kept to a minimum during scene one.*

As Will falls through the large hole, he falls lower and lower. He becomes aware of the thick green light following him down into the blackness of the hole.

His clothes are forced over his face and head as he falls. He tries to pull down his shirt so that he can see where he is going. This he finds difficult to do. He becomes aware that his fingers and toes have gone numb with the coldness and speed at which he is travelling!

He lands and tries to adjust to his new surroundings.

Will, suddenly becomes aware of the green shape of a space being emerging! Straining his eyes, Will glances in the direction of the space being!

Will: 'Where will I hide; where will I run to; how can I escape from this?'

Narrator: Will looks around the large black hole he has landed in. He sees many large, strange, green shapes emerging.

Stage
  Direction: Ziob makes herself known to Will. If made, the large geometric shapes may be brought onto the stage at this point. The green geometric shapes move in and around a softly lit stage.

Will: (Assertively) 'Hello, I'm Will Jones and I live on the island of Ozimoth.'

Ziob,   (Assuredly) 'I'm Ziob, a Space Master.'

Will: (Assertively) 'May I ask, why we are down in this hole within the Planet of Grigan together?'

Ziob: 'We are here to work together. We are here to prepare the children for their next lessons in learning.'

Stage
Direction: *The stage lighting can become lighter and*
              lighter

Narrator: Will listens with interest to Ziob's words.
              Slowly she turned and lifted her sword
              into the black air of Grigan's deep inner
              space. A gentle green light began to glow
              from the sword and the black space
              became lighter, then brighter and
              brighter than anything Will had ever
              seen. He was now seeing a brilliant green-
              lit area deep within the central core of
              Grigan's planet.

Ziob: 'You are now within the City of Epahs,
              which exists deep down within the centre
              of the Planet of Grigan.'

Narrator: Ziob takes a big breath before
              continuing.

Ziob: 'The Space Masters know that thinking
              now is different to what it was many
              generations ago. We need to think of new
              ways and to help people think of new ways

about their problems during this moons'
down and suns' up time.'

Will: (Will thinks a bit before answering) 'I
             have heard my Grandma say, 'Oh, we used
             to think differently in our day!'

Narrator: Will continues to listen, with interest, to
             what Ziob has to say.

Ziob: (Continues) 'We also know that the people
             of the our planet want to trade with
             other planets, and to do this, they need
             to be educated in commerce and trade.'

Stage
Direction: *A burst of green light highlights the
             entire stage.*
             *Many children continue to walk in and
             around the large green geometric shapes
             on the stage and sing:* The Part Song.

Chorus: '1 p, 2 p's, 3 p's, Four
             Counting money makes many, many more;
             1 p, 2 p's 3 p's, Four
             Taking care of my money brings so much
             more.

1 p, 2 p's, 3 p's, Four
Knowing how to work and knowing how to save
1 p, 2 p's, 3 p's, Four'.

End of Scene One

Scene Two:

Narrator: Will meets Chet and the people from the Planet of Zadril.

This scene takes place within the Library and in the City of Epahs on the Planet of Zadril.

(Background): Will is introduced to Chet. Chet is Ziob's scribe who is always busily working on projects for Ziob. Will's attention is taken from Chet and Ziob as he looks at a group of purple people in the far distant corner of the library.

Stage
Direction: *Ziob, Chet and Will are in the Library within the City of Epahs. Chet, Ziob and Will are standing together in front of Chet's work. A group of Purple Lizard people are standing in a distant corner of the library; they are so far away, that Will cannot see their faces.*

Will:	(Will, turning his attention from the Purple Lizard People, speaks to Chet) 'Why do you need to know so much?'
Chet:	(Looks in astonishment at Will) 'Why would you not want to know?'
Stage Direction:	*The library is a busy place with scribes and workers working hard.*
Narrator:	The Space Masters and their scribes are searching for knowledge, ideas and looking for new inventions. Will, now finds he is walking towards where the Lizard People were once standing in the library.
Stage Direction:	*Will sits on a green stone stall and reads from an old manuscript that he finds on the floor.*
Will:	(Reads out loud to the audience) *The Lizard People were once a very wealthy and knowledgeable race.*
	Through laziness, they forgot how to read and learn. Their laziness was so great that the Lizard People of Zadril started to

lose their respect for each other and their planet.

'For generations the people have lived like this. They do not care about the planet or about each other and slowly there have become fewer and fewer people living and fewer babies born on the planet.

'As space time went by, the lazy Lizard People of Zadril used up all of the natural resources of their planet.

The children do not go to school and cannot read; they do not know how to work; they cannot work out simple sums, and nor can they solve simple problems!'

Stage Direction: Will looks up and sees many Space Masters, carrying green swords, walking towards him.
Will suddenly drops the old manuscript onto the floor.

Stage Direction: Will is startled by so many Space Masters standing before him.

Senior Space Master:	'Welcome to Epahs, Will. I see you have been reading about the Lizard People of Zadril. It is very unfortunate, their situation has come about because they did not plan to work for their future; they have become a very lazy race. Our children here too in the City of Epahs are becoming lazy and this is why we have brought you down to our inner city. We would like you to talk to our Space Masters and they can explain to our children how you work on Ozimoth.'
Stage Direction:	*Once the Space Masters have spoken to Will, they turn and walk away.*
Narrator:	Will feels very honoured to be asked to speak to the Space Masters, but he is still very interested in the Lizard People from the Planet of Zadril.

Stage Direction:	While Will is thinking, a small Lizard girl enters the Library and comes up to Will and grabs his hand.
Small Lizard Girl:	'Come with me, my people want to talk to you!'
Stage Direction:	The lighting is dimmed and Will and the small Lizard Girl walk off the stage. End of Scene Two

Scene Three:

Narrator: Will meets the Lizard People from the
            Planet of Zadril and they take a
            hazardous journey!

            There are two parts to this scene. The
            first part takes place outside the
            spaceship and the second part is within
            the spaceship.

Stage
Direction: *Lighting is kept very dim throughout this
            scene. Rubbish is spread all over the
            stage.*

Stage
Direction: *Walking once around the stage.*

Narrator: Will and the small Lizard Girl walk and
              walk for a long time. The weather is very
              cold. The Lizard Girl does not have any
              shoes to wear and is only wearing a light
              dress.

Will: 'Aren't you cold little girl?'

Narrator: The small Lizard girl looks at Will and
              does not answer; she continues to hold
              Will's hand while they walk over rocky,
              cold ground.

Stage
Direction: *Slowly, the Purple Lizard People make
              their way onto the far corner of the
              stage. A Lizard Woman walks over to the
              girl and Will and welcomes them.*

Lizard
Woman: 'Welcome to our place on this planet.'

Stage
Direction: *Will looks around at the bedraggled
              Lizard People.*

Will:	(Replies to the Lizard Woman). 'Chet the Scribe to Ziob, has told me a little bit about your planet.'
Stage Direction:	*The Lizard woman looks at Will through her squinting yellow eyes as he made his last comment. (He then realises quickly he needs to say something)*
Will:	(Hurriedly) 'What is it you want to speak to me about?'
Lizard Woman:	'We want to know how to grow crops; how other people look after their planets; how they live and how they work. We would like to take you to our Planet of Zadril.'
Will:	(Astonishment!) 'When?'
Lizard Woman:	'We are going now.'

Stage Direction:	*The Zadrilian People walk off the stage with Will and the little Lizard girl following behind.*
Narrator:	Will followed the group of Lizard People and knew he should not go with them to the Planet of Zadril, but knew somehow he had too. As the group walk, great, freezing planetary winds blow large lumps of freezing ice into the air.
Stage Direction:	*The group of Lizard People and Will, duck and dive all over the stage as they try to miss the ice hitting them.*
Narrator:	The group of Lizard People now make their way to the waiting spaceship.
Stage Direction:	*The little Lizard girl continues to hold Will's hand throughout this scene.*
Narrator:	Will becomes a reluctant passenger. He now sees how old and rusty the outside and inside the spaceship really is.

Part Two: The group of Lizard People and Will are now within the old, rusty spaceship.

Stage Direction: *Will looks around at the rusty old spaceship, scratches his head as he notices the rusty wires and dials hanging out of the ceiling and walls. Also, the spaceship is very dirty with litter and rubbish pilled up in corners*

Will: 'I'm seriously wondering now if I've made the right decision to go to Zadril?'

Narrator: Crank, crank, crunk, crank, crank the spaceship groans and moans as it tries to fly through space.

Stage Direction: *The Lizard People and Will need to now walk around the stage in a swaying motion (as if they are travelling through space.)*

Will: 'I didn't even imagine that such old spaceships existed in the space worlds. How does this thing fly? There are rusty wires and dials hanging out of the walls; it's a wonder that anything works at all!'

17

Stage Direction:	*Still holding his hand, the Little Lizard girl shows Will around the spaceship.*
Narrator:	The Little Lizard girl introduces the Lizard Woman, her mother to Will.
Will:	(As Will is introduced) 'Is this your teacher?'
Little Lizard Girl:	'Yes, she is also my mother and the Queen of the Lizard People of Zadril. Her name is Queen Irdzla.'
Will:	(Astonishment) 'Then you are a princess!'
Princess:	'Yes, I am, my name is Princess Eex.'
Narrator:	Will scratches his head as he looks at the two scruffy Lizard People standing in front of him and thinks, 'They don't really look like royalty!'

Suddenly, the spaceship makes some unfamiliar noises: crank, crank, groan, bump, bump, bump and crank again.

End of Scene Three

Scene Four:

Narrator: The Zadrilian Space People learn the value of working.

This scene takes place within the old, worn out, rusty spaceship.

The spaceship's engines stop and the group of Lizard people and Will are left floating in space. Will, soon realises, if something isn't done, they will all die in space.

Stage
Direction: *The rubbish is left on the floor for this scene.*

The curtains open with the Zadrilian People and Will appearing to be drifting through space. (they can give the appearance of drifting by walking very slowly and deliberately and slowly moving their arms in an up and down direction.)

20

*Will moves his body in a swimming action
and makes his way, (through space) to
the engine room.*

Will: (While moving and picking up a rusty dial
or a broken spaceship engine part.) 'If
I'm right, these rusty wires and dials
belong back in the walls of the spaceship!

Stage
Direction: *Will looks for something that resembles
a screwdriver.*

Will: 'Ah, that looks like something I could use
as a screwdriver; that's just what I need.'

Narrator: Will, makes himself very busy: he screws
loose screws back into the wall and mends
loose wires that had been hanging out of
the walls of the spaceship.

The Lizard People, including the Queen,
watch him and then start working with
Will, mending, fixing and putting together
dials, wires.

Will and Princess Eex, Queen Irdzla and the Lizard People work hard repairing the spaceship.

Stage
Direction: *The children may need to be shown pieces of equipment such as old parts of washing machines; they may also need an explanation about tools, for instance: What do you use a screwdriver for?*

Will: (Speaking to Princess Eex) 'This old spaceship is very different to the engines of cars and boats and motor bikes that I've worked on with my dad!'

Stage
Direction: *Princess Eex listens to Will, nods her head. All of the people on the spaceship continue to work hard repairing the ship.*

Narrator: Will, looks surprised as he notices: not only are the Lizard People helping to repair the spaceship but they are also picking up the rubbish in the spaceship.

Suddenly, they hear: the sound of the spaceship's engines come to life: crank, groan, crank, crank, crankcrank, whire, whirring, whirring sounds and suddenly, the spaceship is speeding through space on its way to the Planet of Zadril.

Will: 'The people of Zadril look happy after doing the work, Princess Eex.'

Stage
Direction: *The Lizard People chat and slowly walk around the stage as the spaceship takes them on their journey to the Planet of Zadril.*

               Princess Eex is eager to show Will her school work.

Princess
Eex: 'Look Will, look Will, this is all of my school work.'

Stage
Direction: *Princess Eex continues to unravel vast quantities of her school work. All of the*

work is on old, once used paper.(brown paper cut into large pieces would be ideal for this scene.)

As Princess Eex is showing Will her school work, Queen Irdzla explains:

Queen
Irdzla: 'The Space Masters' allow us to use their library; this way we can learn. If our children and our people are to survive, they must be educated and they must know how money works.'

Stage
Direction: *The spaceship is about to land on the Planet of Zadril.*
Will, moves to the spaceship window.

Narrator: By this time, the old spaceship is closer to the Planet of Zadril and Will can see the looming size of the planet.

The ship docks in the landing bay. The doors open: the shrieking hinges scream more and more as the doors are pushed further and further apart. Will then sees rundown buildings and a planet that looks as though it has just been through a war.

On the horizon Will can see the colours of blue and green and says to Princess Eex.

Will: 'I can see the familiar colours of Grigan, Spectron and Ozimoth.

(Will thinks and say out loud) 'Oh dear, I've forgotten about Ben. I was to meet him and I'm now out somewhere in Space. I can't even text him!'

Stage
Direction: *Will feels in his jeans' pocket for his mobile phone.*

Will: 'Drat, I left my mobile phone at home this morning! I couldn't even text Will if I wanted too. We are so far out in space. It would be too far from here, anyway!'

Stage Direction:	As the scene comes to a close: the Lizard People leave the ship. Will notices how they are talking and laughing and enjoying each other's company.
Will:	(Will speaks to Queen Irdzla) 'I can't believe these are the same people who boarded the ship with me; your Majesty, they were so miserable. I wonder if it was learning to work again that has made a difference in their lives?'
Stage Direction:	Queen Irdzla, Princess Eex and Will are the last to leave. The Queen and Princess are busy picking up the precious brown parchments from the dirty ship's floor. The Queen looks up as Will makes his last comment.
Queen Irdzla:	'It may be Will!'

End of Scene Four

Scene Five:

In the dungeons of the Palace of Zadril, Princess Eex meets her Ancient Ancestors and the Messenger.

Background: Scene five takes place in the Palace that is in the City of Lardiz on the Planet of Zadril.

This scene has two parts.

Narrator: Will and Queen Zadrila venture on a mission to find the Wise Ones called the Zarwids of Zadril. Queen Irdzla knows that these Wise Ones hold the secrets to the success of the Lizard People. The Lizard People have not taken any notice of the Wise Ones in the past and this is why they are now hungry, dirty and have no money or education.

The scene opens with Princess Eex, Little Brother and the Zadrilian Butler in the large brown room, the Queen's Apartments, of the Palace. Will and Queen Irdzla are walking out of the scene to start their journey to find the Zarwids.

Princess
Eex   (As Will leaves the scene) 'Look Will, look at my work.'

Will: 'I will look at it when I return.'

Stage
Direction: *Will has almost left the stage when he says.*

Will: 'Princess Eex just wants to know so much and she is so eager to learn everything that she can!'

Stage Direction:	*Princess Eex and Little Brother make themselves very busy as they sit on the floor of the stage. They do many sums and work happily while the old Zadrilian Butler sits in his large, brown stone chair resting.*
Princess Eex:	'Zadrilian Butler, my mother has told me about the dungeons under the palace. I know there are some old parchments down there and I need more parchments to work on.'
Narrator:	Princess Eex will be in big trouble if she is to go to the dungeons under the Palace of Zadril. The dungeon is the burial site of her ancestors and '....should not be disturbed,' her mother had always said.
Zadrilian Butler:	We will both get into very great trouble if we go into the dungeons, you know that, Princess Eex.'

Princess Eex:	(Persistently to the Zadrilian Butler.) 'Oh, please Butler, please let's go down to the dungeons, please, please come with me!'
Narrator:	In the end, to get some peace, the Elderly Butler had no choice but to go down to the dungeons.
Stage Direction:	*The lights are dimmed. Little Brother moves discretely off the stage. Princess Eex and the Elderly Butler slowly walk down the large stone steps into the dungeon.*
	Children can mime walking down the steps with slow, deliberate steps and using their arms to balance their steps. This movement will give the impression of walking down large stairs.
Xannts:	'Snap, Snap, Snap, Snap, Snap, Snap.'
Stage	

Direction: The Xannnts continually snap during the time the Princess and the Butler are in the dungeon.

Narrator: Snapping Xannnts continually frighten the Princess by snapping at her legs and head. The Princess and Butler are continuously wiping large cobwebs from their faces. They both feel they want to turn back and go to the comfort of the Palace. The Princess, however, is determined to find what she is looking for: parchment to do her school work on!

Princess
Eex: 'Look Butler, there may be some parchments over there.'

(Excitedly) 'Look Butler, look Butler, what are those shapes over there?'

Zadrilian Butler:	'I think they may be your ancestors, Princess Eex, but I'm not entirely sure! You know you should not disturb your ancestors, Princess Eex!'
Stage Direction:	*Princess Eex feels a little guilty.*
Princess Eex:	'I don't want to disturb my ancestors, but I need the parchment to work on and this is the only place I know that I can get it.'
Narrator:	At the end of a large corridor, Princess Eex suddenly sees a pile of old manuscripts, books and old parchments. She runs to the pile. She starts searching through the pile looking for anything that she can use to do her schoolwork on.
Princess Eex:	'Look Butler, look at all of these books and paper!'

Stage
Direction: The Xannnts continue snapping, snapping,
             snapping.

             Both the Princess and the Butler are so
             busy looking at the writings, old
             manuscripts and old parchments - they
             don't notice what happens next! The
             Butler suddenly sees an unfamiliar figure
             standing next to one of the Ancient
             Ancestors

Xannnts
continue: 'Snap, snapsnapsnap, snap, snap, snap.'

Stage
Direction: The Elderly Lizard Butler fell to his
             knees as he realised who was standing
             before him. The Intergalactic Space
             Master moves from the shadows of the
             stage into full light.

Intergalactic
Space
Master: 'I am here as a messenger from King
             Lagrieb. Elderly Zadrilian Butler, you

must help Princess Eex all you can. Then, you will find the parchment you are looking for.'

Stage
Direction: *The lights dim. In an instant the Messenger had disappeared. After seeing the Messenger, the Zadrilian Butler is unable to think: he stands scratching his head until he can think clearly.*

Princess Eex and the Butler then continue searching for the parchment.

Narrator: 'For some reason, the Butler glanced in the direction of one of the ancestor's whose 'mummified' eyes appeared to be looking at him!

The Butler then felt 'goose bumps' run down his spine as he realised it one of the Kings of Ancients' past!'

Zadrilian Butler:	'Princess Eex, I do believe that I just saw the eyes of one of the Ancient's moving and twitching!'
Princess Eex:	(Grabbing the Butler's hand) 'Do you really think so, Butler?'
Stage Direction:	*The lights dim and rolls of white parchment tied with purple and gold ribbon are put at the feet (as though appearing) of the Ancient Ancestor.* *Princess Eex and the Zadrilian Butler cautiously move over to where the Ancient Ancestor is standing.*
Princess Eex:	'There is so much parchment appearing that I will have enough to work on for the rest of my life and I will be able to give the parchment to all the children of Zadril!'

Stage
Direction: *The lights are dimmed as Princess Eex*
and the Zadrilian Butler bend down and
collect armfuls each of the gleaming,
white parchment.

End of Scene Five

Scene Six:

Ziob, the Space Master, visits Princess Eex. .

Stage
Direction: *The scene opens with Princess Eex and*
            Ziob standing, looking at each other, on
            the brown stone floor (in the Queen's
            Apartments) of the Palace of Zadril.

Narrator: Princess Eex and the Zadrilian Butler had
            walked for many Zadrilian hours up and
            down the dungeon steps carrying armfuls
            of white parchment all tied with purple
            and gold ribbons.

            The Butler, who is now very tired, sits in
            his brown stone chair and falls into a
            deep sleep. Little Brother too, is sleeping
            on the brown stone floor.

            While Ziob is looking for Will Jones, she
            visits Princes Eex in the Palace on the
            Planet of Zadril. Meanwhile, Will Jones is
            on a journey to find the Zarwids, the
            Wise Ones, with Queen Irdzla of Zadril.

Direction: *If possible, a green light needs to search around the stage at the entrance of Ziob, The Space Master.*

Ziob, is now standing before Princess Eex and bends down to touch the arm of the Princess.

Princess
Eex: (Frightened) Screams once.

Ziob: 'I am Ziob from the City of Epahs. Please do not be frightened, little Princess Eex, we are looking for Will Jones.'

(Ziob continues.) 'What are you doing?

Princess
Eex: 'I'm working and trying to complete as many sums and mathematical parchments as I can, to show Will when he returns.'

Narrator: 'Princess Eex is trying to act very brave and grown-up in front of Ziob, but she

could feel her knees start to shake as
she speaks.

Stage
Direction: Both Ziob and the Princess sit on the
              brown stone floor and start to work on
              the mathematical questions and answers.

Princess
Eex:,   .'One, Two, Three, Four Xannnts.'

Stage
Direction: Princess Eex has drawn many Xannnts on
              her parchments. She has been doing some
              arithmetic. She has multiplied Xannnts,
              taken away Xannnt and worked out the
              numbers that are left over.

(Children will need to be familiar with the parchments in the resource pack to fully understand what the Princess is doing.)

Princess
Eex: 'I'm now doing multiplication of Xannnts and some take away sums of Xannnts.'

Stage
Direction: *Princess Eex busies herself working. While she is working she suddenly says to Ziob.*

Princess
Eex: 'I've heard our Butler speak about money that our people used to use before we started to live like we do now. Do you use money on your planet?'

Stage
Direction: *Princess Eex, continues to work on her parchments, not looking at Ziob while Ziob answers her.*

Ziob: 'Yes, we do.

Princess Eex:	'What planet do you live on Ziob?'
Ziob:	'I live on the Planet of Grigan in the City of Epahs.'
Princess Eex:	'What work do you do on the Planet of Grigan?'
Ziob:	'I am a Space Master and I work in the Treasury of Epahs. I look after the money of our City. I have to make sure that we only spend the money we have in the Treasury. (Ziob continues) 'We have many Space Masters on Epahs. We all have different jobs to do.

'Because I look after the money of Epahs, the government of Epahs pays me money in return for my work.' |
| Stage Direction: | Ziob gives a little chuckle and then a giggle. |

Ziob: (Continues) 'I'm paid money to look after
                 money! Funny that, isn't it? I'm paid
                 money to look after money!'

Narrator: 'Princess Eex looks at Ziob's face and
                 realised that even Ziob was a little
                 confused about being paid money to look
                 after money!'

Ziob: 'I have to make sure we pay our bills on
                 time and that we have enough money and
                 that we don't run out of money: and
                 that's my job!

Stage
Direction: *Ziob scratches her chin and thinks for a
                 moment.*

Ziob: 'I have to balance the books, so to speak!'

                 (Ziob continues) 'On other planets, when
                 the space people work for the King or
                 Queen or the government or for
                 somebody, they have to pay the people
                 for the work they have done.'

Narrator: 'The Princess had never heard of this
             before and asks:

Princess
Eex: 'What is pay?'

Ziob: 'Pay or payment is given to you if you
             work for somebody or for the
             government. For instance, and when you
             become a Queen, you may ask one of your
             citizens to clean the streets. If you do
             not offer them payment for their work,
             they will not want to clean the streets, so
             you city will become dirty!'

             (Ziob continues) 'Do you understand
             Princess Eex?'

Princess
Eex: 'Is that why our streets are so dirty?'

Narrator: 'Listening carefully to the question, Ziob
             changes the conversation.

Ziob: I'm now going to show you how our money
             system works in the City of Epahs.'

Stage
Direction: *Ziob remains sitting on the floor with the*
               full concentration of Princess Eex. Ziob
               continues to draw many coins on the
               white parchments.

               The lights dim

               End of Scene Six

Scene Seven:

The Elderly Zadrilian Butler shows Princess Eex and Little Brother how money works.

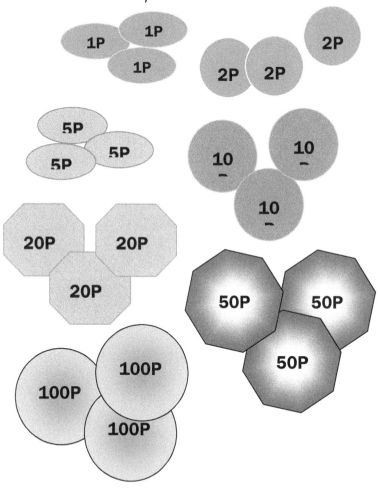

Stage
Direction: *The final scene opens with Ziob and*
              Princess Eex sitting on the floor of the
              Palace. They had been working for many
              sun ups and moon downs – all of the time,
              Little Brother and the Elderly Zadrilian
              Butler, continue to sleep.

Ziob: 'Here we have the coins we use in Epahs:
              1 p, 2 p's, 3 p's, 5 parts, 10 p's, 20 p's, 50
              p's and 100 p's.

              Our children sing a song that helps them
              to remember how to work with money.
              Now let me sing this song to you.'

Stage
Direction: *Ziob now starts to sing with the chorus.*

Chorus: 1 p, 2 p's, 3 p's, Four
              Counting money makes many, many more;
              1 p, 2 p's 3 p's, Four
              Tacking care of my money brings so much
              more.

              1 p, 2 p's, 3 p's, Four

Knowing how to work and knowing how to save gives me satisfaction in 1 p, 2 p's, 3 p's, Four.

<table>
<tr><td>Stage Direction:</td><td>Princess Eex sits listening; at the end of the song she claps her hands.</td></tr>
</table>

Ziob: 'In Epahs, a shape is the whole amount and if we have one hundred p's in our money, we have one shape to spend. We use shapes and p's as our money. Money is also called currency.

Narrator: 'Princess Eex is so excited about what she is learning, she has forgotten about Little Brother and the elderly Zadrilian Butler are still fast asleep!'

Stage Direction: Princess Eex is working hard doing sums on her clean, white parchments. The lights are dimmed and Ziob swirls around and around and disappears off the stage. Princess Eex, because she is so busy does not know her new friend has vanished into thin air!

The Elderly Zadrilian Butler and Little Brother are now awake. The Butler is confused and bewildered by the amount of work he sees on the floor. He scratches his head in disbelief!

Zadrilian
Butler: 'Did you do all that work while I was asleep?'

Princess
Eex: 'Yes, well, somebody helped me!'

*Stage
Direction
&*
Narrator: The Butler looks very carefully at all of the parchments the Princess has been working on. He scratches his head again and looks in wonderment at such very good work!

Zadrilian
Butler: 'My, you have been busy.'

Narrator:	'The Elderly Zadrilian Butler thinks to himself: "I remember money. We used to use it, and it made working much more enjoyable. It was nice to be appreciated and to be paid fairly for what I did." '
Princess Eex:	'Butler, please tell me how money used to be used on Zadril?'
Zadrilian Butler:	(He hesitates before answering the Princess) 'This is the value of money and how it works.'
Stage Direction:	*The Butler draws large round coins on parchments.*
	Little Brother shows some interest.
Little Brother:	'What do you do with those things?'
Zadrilian Butler:	'We use them to buy things.'

Little
Brother: 'I don't understand.'

Zadrilian
Butler: 'Children, many, many generations ago
              used to play ball but now, they don't do
              much of anything! Now, if you could buy a
              ball, would you?'

Stage
Direction: *Both children shout their answers.*

Little
Brother: 'Yes, yes.'

Princess
Eex: 'Yes, yes, of course.'

Direction: *The Zadrilian Butler draws many*
wonderful things on the white parchment.

Zadrilian
Butler: 'Just suppose you want to buy a drum
from your friend. Your friend says, "It
will cost you 50 p's." You have 60 p's in
your pocket. If the drum cost 50 p's, you
will have 10 p's change from your friend.
Do you understand?'

Little
Brother: (Hesitates) 'I think so!'

Princes
Eex: 'Yes, yes, I understand. You have more
money than the drum costs so you get 10
p's back.

Zadrilian
Butler: 'Excellent, you have the idea.'

'Now what is the most favourite thing in
your whole life, Little Brother?'

Stage Direction:	*Little Brother doesn't need to think too hard or long and shouts:*
Little Brother:	'Icen cones, icen cones, I just love icen cones.'
Stage Direction:	*The Zadrilian Butler thinks for a while and then says:*
Zadrilian Butler:	(Remorseful) 'Yes, it's a long time since we had icen cones!'
	(Enthusiastically) 'If you had 40 p's and the icen cone cost you 25 p's, how much change would you get?'
Stage Direction:	*Little Brother starts working the sum out on his fingers and says:*
Little Brother:	'I haven't got enough fingers to work that sum out – it's too big for me to do.'

Princess Eex:	'I know, I know, it's 15 p's change.
Zadrilian Butler:	'Excellent, excellent, Princess Eex and well done Little Brother for trying so hard.'
Stage Direction:	At that point, Will and Queen Irdzla return from their trip to the Zarwids.
Narrator	The Queen now looks at the parchments. She is overcome by the amount of work Princess Eex has done in her absence.
Stage Direction:	The Queen falls to her knees and cries. Both of the children run to her and the three sit together on the floor of the stage. Will and the Zadrilian Butler look on.
	The lighting of the stage is dimmed.

Princess Eex, Little Brother, Queen Irdzla and the Zadrilian Butler change into their royal clothes and the face paint is removed.

The stage lights come up for the final but brief scene.

Queen
Irdzla: 'We are now back to the way we were many generations ago. The Empress of Zarwid has told me:

"Your people need to work but they must be rewarded. Your ancestors would pay the people for the work they did. For generations the leaders of the City of Lardiz have not paid for the work that was done by the people. Your people now have no heart to work: they have lost the 'gift of life' and that is why you must change the way you work with your people. When people work they must be rewarded.'

End of Scene Seven – End Of The Play.
The cast join Queen Irdzla, Princess Eex, Little
Brother and the Zadrilian Butler on the stage for the
finale; it's optional to conclude the song:

Chorus:　　'1 p, 2 p's, 3 p's, Four
　　　　　　Counting money makes many, many more;
　　　　　　1 p, 2 p's 3 p's, Four
　　　　　　Taking care of my money brings so much
　　　　　　more.
　　　　　　1 p, 2 p's, 3 p's, Four
　　　　　　Knowing how to work and knowing how to
　　　　　　save
　　　　　　1 p, 2 p's, 3 p's, Four'.

Ozimoth Money

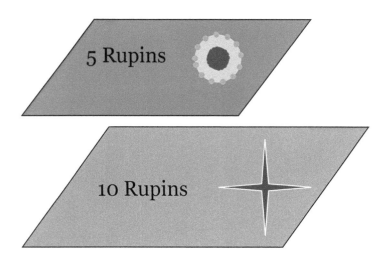

5 Rupins

10 Rupins

Zadrilian Money

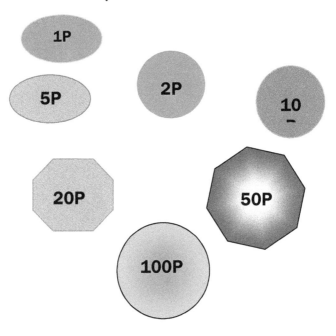

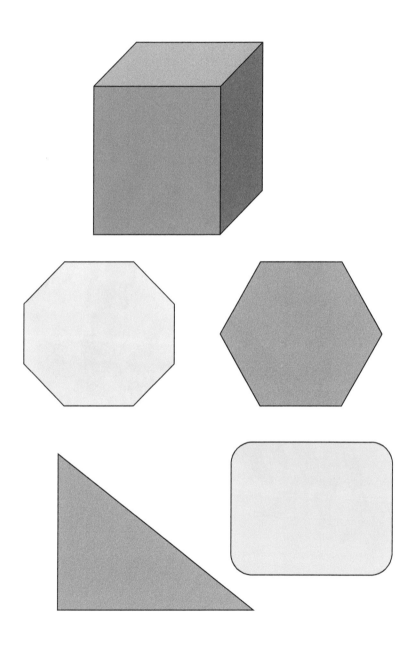

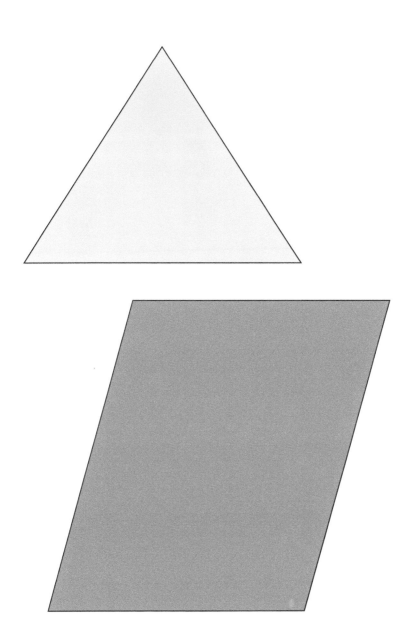

CPSIA information can be obtained
at www.ICGtesting.com
Printed in the USA
BVHW021757240221
601018BV00014B/126